Love
On Me

Picking up the Broken Pieces to Heal
and Become Renewed

By

Sheldine Gordon

Love On Me

© 2021 by Sheldine Gordon

All rights reserved. No portion of this publication may be reproduced, stored in a retrieval system, or transmitted in any form or by any means–electronic, mechanical, photocopying, recording, scanning, or other–except for brief quotations in critical reviews or articles, without the prior written permission of the publisher.

Published in Hampton, VA, by Fruition Publishing Concierge Services. Fruition Publishing Concierge Services is a division of Alesha Brown, LLC.

Fruition Publishing Concierge Services can bring authors to your live event. For more information or to book an event, visit Fruition Publishing Concierge Services at

www.FruitionPublishing.com

ISBN: 978-1-954486-15-7 Paperback
ISBN: 978-1-954486-16-4 eBook
Library of Congress Control Number: 2021912958

DEDICATION

This book is dedicated, with love, to my children, Kershel and Keron, who have been my driving force to succeed and, most importantly, not give up as a single mom.

Thank you, God, for the opportunity to write my story. My family, especially my cousin Sharon, your love and support are highly treasured and are irreplaceable. I can count on you for almost anything.

To my daughter and son, thank you for your unwavering support and love for me, even though things were sometimes hard. I regret all the pain and disappointments you have experienced. I pray that you will both be the best version of yourselves and continue to trust in God always.

To my photographer Kelon Miller, you captured that beautiful moment very well. To my beautiful, talented stylist Dr. Nicola Ifill-Fraser, I appreciate all you did last minute in coordinating my wardrobe. Thank you to all the people who encouraged me, sent messages, testimonials, or contributed in any way to make this book a reality.

Thank you to all my prayer partners from my church ministry. Friends and sisters in Christ, Yvette Francois Joseph, Katherine Bethel, Arlene Villarule, Kerry Ann Duncan, your daily posts and blogs are always uplifting and encouraging to my spirit and a constant reminder of God's love through scriptures.

Table of Contents

Love Changed Me "The Re-Introduction"	1
Living Together, Learning, and Experiencing Life's Challenges	15
Love On Me	23
Processing, Healing, and Reconnecting	35
Breathe and Exhale	47
Patience and Peace	59
Great Momentum	67
Growth, New Adventures, and Being Intentional	77
Finally Loving On Me	93
Meet the Author	97

Featured Guest Contributors:

Simone N. Bharath	101
Dr. Deena Brown	105
Neisha Guy	109
Noreen N. Henry	113
Monica Reed	117
Vernae Taylor	121

Love Changed Me
"The Re-Introduction"

In Guyana, on the South-Eastern shores of South America, lived a beautiful young lady. She lived with her *rich* uncle (or so they said). Her dad lived overseas and was not married to her mom. Her mom lived in Guyana but decided to have her stay with her uncle as he was financially able to assist her with her school and daily expenses.

The beautiful young lady in Guyana had access to everything she needed while growing up. EVERYTHING (or so they said): a big house, vehicles, money, travels, and love.

Her aunty was ambitious, intelligent, glamorous, loving, and full of fun. Her uncle had no children and made everything she needed accessible. They were admired, especially her uncle, who always worked hard to make his family's life *comfortable*. Life with her uncle and aunty was the life she imagined she would have as an adult.

But the fact remained that her parents were not together. The need for a husband like her uncle, with all his qualities, was the beautiful young lady's desire.

At age 18, she started her first job in the retail industry while she lived with her uncle, learning financial management. She saved and bought the things she needed. She also contributed to the home, even if it was a small amount.

Feeling all grown up, her eyes looked for the "charms" of a good man. Although she was 18, according to her cultural customs, permission was needed to go on dates and to clubs. Some of the young men interested in her were not approved to date her. Even though she had access to almost everything, the freedom to choose her friends and go out were sometimes an issue for her uncle.

The beautiful young lady decided to go on a vacation at her favorite cousin's home in Barbados. The vacation felt like freedom. She went out with cousins, made new friends, started to date, worked, and did some small modeling gigs. All of those activities were enjoyed without having to ask for permission. She thought about not returning to Guyana, regardless of her immigration status. However, six months later, Guyana became her home once again.

She was sad to leave the wonderful young man that she had started dating. He was ambitious and focused. The two had managed their expenses well, loved each other, and were both sociable. Independence was her biggest luxury while she lived in Barbados.

Back in Guyana, the beautiful young lady felt uncomfortable and decided to go to Trinidad. In December 1999, her suitcase was packed and a holiday to Trinidad was set.

At first, life in Trinidad was a challenge for her since she didn't have any immediate family or friends there. She kept in mind all of her uncle's qualities and hoped to find the perfect partner. She wanted an ambitious, financially stable, wonderful, and fun-loving man. Life in Trinidad didn't bring any of that.

Instead, she found a partner who mentioned *love*. He was simple and practically had nothing: no fancy cars, no big house, and no money.

Her perspective in life changed as her situation and experiences changed. She challenged herself to just trust love and forget all about the glamor of material things. She started dating while working at a casino in Trinidad.

She got intimate with her new love and was pregnant in 2002 with a beautiful baby girl. The two married two years later and conceived their second child, a son, five years later. But married life proved to be full of ups and downs.

Ups and downs were actually serious problems including physical abuse which eventually led to divorce. After divorce, the beautiful young lady looked at life as growing lessons, lots of changes, and nothing like the *fairy tale* stories of her youth. She decided to be strong and focused on building herself financially and emotionally.

For a while, the beautiful young lady was free from setbacks. She had a small circle of friends and a great support team comprised of her mom and family who lived in Guyana while she lived and worked in Trinidad. Although it was the best decision for her at the time, the change affected her emotionally and mentally.

Not being able to do things with her children or nurture them as a full-time mom deeply saddened her. The distance between them also affected the children. It was difficult for them to adjust to the new country, culture, and school while missing both of their parents.

Life became harder each day as her income now had to cover rent, daily expenses, and money to send back home to Guyana. Eventually, the beautiful young lady took two jobs to make ends meet, determined to get over the hurdle.

She started work in retail in 2010 and a part-time job at a restaurant in the evenings. This increased her finances so much so that she traveled frequently to Guyana to visit the children. Her life became manageable and she started to date again, went out, played mass (carnival), fashion modeled, and enjoyed life to the fullest.

One year later, while playing mass, she felt strange. She no longer wanted to be in the band and left instantly. She realized that all the freedom she once enjoyed no longer satisfied her, but she wanted to be loved and cared for more than being free.

The next day, she prayed, talked to God, and went to church (now a frequent habit), and her hobbies changed. Church was such a wonderful experience for her that she gave her life over to God. After being baptized, she felt brand new and free, but this time, that freedom was so different. Trusting in God was the best decision. She smiled and became content, even without the material things.

About two years later, an old friend started to chat with her online. They were happy to reconnect even though it was not a physical connection. They talked each day on the phone or online and eventually opened up about their current status, both divorced. The friendship developed over some months; they shared many similarities in terms of life perspectives and serving God. Her new *boyfriend* traveled to Trinidad a minimum of three times a year just to see her.

On her birthday in January, he surprised her with a proposal. She smiled from ear to ear and said YES! One year later, they were married. It was a small wedding, everyone dressed nicely, and the place was decorated like a fairy tale. The groom sang to her too. That day, everything was beautiful.

The honeymoon was great on the beaches of Tobago and they explored the beautiful island. Her husband returned to the U.S but visited Trinidad frequently.

During the three years of their long-distance relationship/marriage, her husband filed the immigration papers for his new family to join him in the U.S. The process took a while, but they waited patiently and, their love blossomed even more as the anxiousness for them to be together grew more and more.

On April 11, 2017, they traveled to the U.S. where everything was different. The weather, the currency, the food, school, culture, environment, work: EVERYTHING was different.

Day by day, they adapted and managed. The beautiful young lady enjoyed being the full-time mom she desired to be and also a full-time wife. The apartment was small; not the usual setting of everyone having their own room as they did in Guyana or Trinidad. Every space was small in New York.

The children started school while she stayed at home and daily looked for a job. While being a stay-at-home wife and mom, the beautiful young lady's husband was supportive as he saw the discomfort on her face regarding being unemployed. She worried about the bills and her children's care. The search for a job continued as she wanted to contribute and improve their living situation.

During that time, her husband informed them of the *rules* while staying there and the eventful happenings in New York. Each day seemed longer for her while staying home with nothing to do. She would sit and wait for the children to come home and tell her about their experiences at school. They laughed and compared life in New York to their former life in Guyana. Her husband made more *rules* and they had no choice but to conform. Each day she prayed and asked God for a job and her prayers were eventually answered.

Adjusting to the culture of New York and its work environment was challenging at first, but the beautiful young lady was once again determined to make the best out of it, for her and her entire family. She contributed to the bills, bought clothes for her and her children, bought furniture, and decorated the apartment using a woman's touch. She felt good even though she had to adhere to the *rules* of the house.

The beautiful young lady placed her energy on all the positives to get through each day. A familiar scene from her past reemerged: her husband soon became abusive and the authorities intervened on three separate occasions.

She tried to be calm and collected at work, on social media, and in church. Her husband had a justification for everything. She worked different shifts and, as a result, she came home each day to numerous complaints about the children.

At first, she thought to herself, *these children are about to mess with my wonderful marriage.* But the thought bothered her. She reached out to a pastor from Trinidad for advice and help. After several one-on-one sessions over several months, things got even worse. Before one year elapsed, her daughter could no longer stay at the apartment due to the abuse. The constant conflict continued.

The beautiful young lady cried many nights and days, even at work, making sure no one saw her. The *rules* continued and she felt overwhelmed. She asked her pastor at the church she attended in Brooklyn to intervene. Counseling sessions were scheduled as the coupled approached one and a half years together in the U.S.

They went to the marriage counseling session twice and her husband said he would not return to speak to *a man* about his problems. The beautiful young lady's husband had lots of controlling ways and religious beliefs which, to him, were always right. The control and verbal abuse of her and her son continued. Somehow, she and her son could do nothing right.

The couple hardly communicated, even though they lived in the same house. Her husband would constantly send messages ordering her around or complaining to her via phone. Finally, one day, he gave her a date to leave the apartment. That came as a complete shock!

The beautiful young lady started to look for apartments based on her income and something that would be close to work. It was a challenge but she remained hopeful. Then, one day, her cousin told her to sublet with her. That brought great relief to her and the two made arrangements as she secured her deposit and rent while setting a date to move.

In July 2019, despite the challenges, the beautiful young lady moved out. She was tired and stressed but thankful to God that He made a way of escape. She was determined not to give up on life and her children's future. She trusted in God even more than before.

Lord, you brought me this far and
I am not giving up.

She even advised other people in similar situations to trust in God for strength and press on.

In January 2020, she was served divorce papers at work. She took a deep breath and, a few days after, signed and mailed them. Each day, with prayers and the support of her family, friends, and a positive network group, the transition became easy. Life continued for her and she felt beautiful, free, and peaceful.

Experiencing the love of God made the divorce pass with ease as it really changed her. She is a stronger person today because of her past experiences. She is not bitter or unforgiving. Everything was done in love and forgiveness. She loved her husband and was loyal to their vows.

As painful as the overall failure of her marriage was, she stands firm today and proclaims that she loves

God, loves herself, and loves her family. Despite everything, her self-worth is intact. She is me, Sheldine Gordon, and I chose to **Love On Me**.

"Brokenness might seem like a bad thing, but it can actually serve a beautiful purpose. Through broken-ness, the outer shell, or the fleshly, ungodly parts of us can be thrown off, and the Character of Christ in our Spirit can shine brighter. As a result, we become more open and available for God to work through us in brand new ways."

- Joyce Meyer

YOUR THOUGHTS

How has love changed you? Think about your past romantic relationships.

_____

_____

_____

_____

_____

_____

What did you learn about love from the relationships you saw in childhood?

_____

_____

_____

_____

_____

Today, how do you define love?

_____

_____

_____

_____

_____

Living Together, Learning, and Experiencing Life's Challenges

"Turn your wounds into wisdom."

- Oprah Winfrey

Over the years, my mom and sisters played a part in raising my children. I assisted with the financial part only. While it was a joy to have the children live with me, it was also a challenge. I challenged myself to be the best mom I could while holding down one to two jobs at a time.

I made major decisions and tried to make time to socialize with them on my days off. Some days, I felt so overwhelmed being a single mom, but God knew it was my heart's desire to have both of my children with me. I had it hard some days, having to make some difficult decisions as I played both mom and dad. Our lives were not a fairy-tale.

I would tell them to do well in school. I urged them to stay focused and aim for the top, to be the best they could be despite the challenges. While trying to adapt in America, aka the *Big Apple,* during the pandemic, I also changed jobs. No, that decision wasn't easy or realistic, but I pressed on and got one.

To many, it looked easy but it was hard on my body. The long working hours and the commute from home to work were taxing. I told my children they needed to be resourceful, responsible, and strong. All I wanted, in return, was for them to be respectful, get good grades in school, and be spiritually grounded in Christ Jesus.

As far back as I could remember, I've always tried to help people in any way I could, but I seldom asked for help. Maybe this is why my friends and family assumed I never needed help. In my mind, I called myself a *Super Mom* as I would sometimes even surprise myself on how I managed our finances to pay the bills, give the children allowances/rewards, and save a little. I was never ashamed of my situation as I knew my truth and my story. I believed I was destined to show my children and others that we can overcome our life's challenges.

> ***"If I can offer any advice, it would be to remain positive! Unless someone has walked in your shoes, no one can nor should judge."***

After being divorced twice, my aim and focus were to be there for my children to help them grow into incredible people. Day by day, my strength was seen while my brokenness healed.

At first, my son was shy and, most of the time, he had low self-esteem. He was living in his shell as a result of experiencing my abusive past. As time went by, I saw him began to open up, expressing himself with lots of compassion and love. He wanted to step up as my big helper. He was finally getting out of his shell. I used that time to teach him what a healthy relationship should be: one full of love, communication, and respect for each other.

My daughter, on the other hand, was a bit rebellious at first. Thank God for the power of prayer! Constant prayer coupled with honest and deep conversations together, we were able to understand each other. Trust me, it wasn't easy.

The process was so hard that sometimes I cried while praying to God. I often cried in my tiny bathroom, where I would be away from everyone at home. But things eventually worked out and I'm always amazed and thankful to God.

My children are my biggest motivators. They help me overcome every time I see them smile with contentment and gratitude. I am also blessed to have the support of my cousins and wonderful friends. Each day, a daily inspirational message or quote, a constant reminder of God's goodness, keeps me strong:

> *"Your big opportunity may be right where you are now."*
>
> *- Napoleon Hill*

Trust is a small word to describe such a big feeling. When trust is broken it shatters, making it almost impossible to put the pieces back together. I have struggled with trust: understanding it, maintaining it, and believing it is possible.

YOUR THOUGHTS

What does trust mean to you?

_____

_____

_____

_____

_____

_____

_____

_____

How would you describe what it is like to trust someone?

_____

_____

_____

_____

_____

Who do you trust 100 percent?

_____

_____

_____

_____

_____

Who is the most non-judgmental person or friend you know?

_____

_____

_____

_____

_____

Who makes up your support team? Who can you run to when you need help?

_____

_____

_____

_____

_____

Have you ever had a person break your trust? Who was it and what did they do?

_____

_____

_____

_____

_____

Visit loveonmebook.com to hear the theme song, Look At Me by Kershel Thomas.

Love On Me

"There is no reason to keep tearing yourself down when God is building you up every day."

- Morgan Harper Nichols

I WILL REJOICE because despite all my struggles and circumstances I still have the love of God in me and now have complete love for myself. I am still joyous and full of life and the freshness of God is within me.

I start my day being thankful and ready for what is in store. I still have that vibrancy and a flare of light in me. Each day I exhibit that newness because my hope is in Christ Jesus.

"God's love is in me so why not Love On Me?"

As I thought of this title, I started to write wholesomely about *myself*. Then, for some reason, I had writer's block. I couldn't get past a paragraph. I know had it not been for God, I would not have had the strength to stand firm today. My own strength was not enough to get me through my divorce.

While I consider my story my testimony, I was prompted by God not to exalt *self* and He helped me to articulate my writing and thoughts in the simplest form.

It is important to **Love On Me**, as I am an overcomer of my circumstances. I didn't get bitter but better. I learned how to let go, embrace the changes in my life positively, and I want others in similar situations to just try my process of this love, **the love of God,** which made me love and appreciate myself.

After my divorce, I checked into myself, like really checked in, and my first destination was my **happiness.** I had to wonder, *was I really happy with myself all those years?*

I needed to accept myself physically and mentally: the thin-boned girl, the girl with the big forehead, my accent, my nationality, my flaws, and my weakness. Recognizing and accepting who I was, proved to be my turning point to greatness. My greatness needed to start from within. Once that was done, I didn't need to use anything or anyone to cover my insecurities.

Sometimes, a bad situation can birth good opportunities. In my struggles after divorce, I found all my insecurities: constantly looking for the love I dreamed of from others; trying to fit into their culture to feel love and gain happiness. None of my actions to pursue the love and acceptance I craved made me happy. Instead, as I checked in with God for answers, I realized that I needed to acknowledge Him, my first love! Having that personal relationship with God is a plus in all this. I am guided along through scriptures and my personal one-on-one talk with God through prayer.

Let me explain….

While I lived with my then-husband, I did not have the full knowledge of God's love even though I was baptized. I basically followed everything and accepted all that my husband told me to do while he quoted scriptures from the Bible. Not having a full personal relationship with God resulted in me giving my husband the power to control and abuse my children and me, all in the name of love.

Some days, after a long day at work, I just wanted to shower and sleep, but he passed judgment on me as I didn't pray how he showed me to pray. I am not against prayer as prayers to God are always necessary. However, my then-husband had structured ways to pray while we lived there. (You know, one of his many *rules*.)

Every time you went outside the door and came back in, even if it was to empty the garbage, you had to pray. While prayers to God are always recommended, if you are tired or forgot, my ex-husband would pass judgment on you. Even in our social activities, he took control of the plans and locations, which made him happy and not me. We needed to wear the outfit he chose or a certain color, sit at a certain table or even laugh a certain way. Everything was tense and a sense of control.

I love being spontaneous sometimes, fun, and love to laugh, which was the total opposite after we married. A lot of activities were curtailed or, for the most part, deemed not important and didn't fit well with my ex-husband's religious beliefs. It's like he wanted to change me to his likeness rather than allow God to change me into His likeness. It was emotionally and mentally draining.

I realized how much I missed in life as I tried to make him and others happy and sought happiness from them over the years. I neglected myself and settled for less of my expectations as I searched for love. After so much hurt, I continued to question myself as to where my true source of love was and how to find it.

I know we all, at some point in our lives, have experienced feelings of discouragement, depression, separation, or divorce, which have caused us to have self-doubt. For me, it was hard to love myself after two failed marriages. People would say, *Sheldine, you look beautiful; I love your smile; you're awesome.* The physical was what everyone saw, but I needed the true sense of love to complete me. Their compliments couldn't fill that void in me. Yes, I was baptized and accepted Jesus in my life but didn't truly understand the fullness of God's love.

While I used the #loveonme and to encourage myself and to accept myself, I was still led away from Jesus. I started to dig deeper into reading and studying God's word: I needed to make time for Him while in my busy schedule of everyday ups and downs. My Bible soon became my new app on my phone. Getting in His word, in worship, and in praise, each day and each moment brought the joy and happiness I longed for.

One morning, as I walked on the sidewalk, I started to praise God openly and, oh, what an awesome feeling that was! I had so much going on at that time, but God! Even then, I felt so much peace.

As I opened my heart to Him, I realized He did not tell us to love ourselves first in order to love well. I needed to love Him first! You need to love Him first!

God calls us to love in a self-sacrificial way. As I filled my spirit each day with His Word, I experienced the unconditional love of God and was able to love myself more.

I am not trying to be religious here; I am just sharing how experiencing a personal relationship with God truly caused me to love myself. I don't need just any **Love On Me**, but God's love on me. Now that's the type of love that will leave you screaming, *yes, love on me*!

Knowing that God sacrificed everything for me to live, even the ways that were viewed and condemned by many, lets me know that I am loved and accepted. God chose me, He loves me, and He took all of my brokenness away.

1 Samuel 16:7, NIV *But the Lord said to Samuel, "Do not consider his appearance or his height, for I have rejected him. The Lord does not look at the things people look at. People look at the outward appearance, but the Lord looks at the heart."*

While I would have loved to brag and boast how I moved on with ease, how my self-love empowered me, it could not give me the satisfaction or fulfillment of God's love. Trust me, I tried it and I spoke it into myself. For so long, I thought I could do it on my own. It wasn't until I truly started to seek the Father, God, that I realized it wasn't my strength but the love of God that was poured into me as I spent quality time with Him. Each moment, I got a better understanding of the depths of God's love and mercy. God's love truly needed to be my top priority, even before me loving myself. I had to exalt Him and not myself.

Today, I will continue to rejoice and can say that I am loved because God is love and His love is on me. **Love On Me**, Lord!

I love helping others, but if I'm going to make the journey ahead, I must learn how to give to myself and receive it. I believe it's important to love oneself as self-introspection is indeed important to one's growth. I needed to identify my problem and why, in most situations and relationships in my life where I felt stuck, I just went through the motions. This feeling was articulated and I knew I needed to do something to help better myself.

I needed to face the fact that what I accepted in my past marriages didn't make me happy. My happiness needed to start within me and God was my first and only source. When I found Him, I started to find myself and each day He taught me something new. He still does.

I pledge (for myself and those that love me):

- To love God unconditionally. By doing so, I am able to get that overflow in myself to respect, accept, and focus on my positive attributes.

- To live in my dreams and not those of others' perceptions.

- To let my yes be yes and not no.

- To be fervently protective of my heart and let God be my guide in all my decision-making, therefore, I will harvest kindness to myself and others.

A sense of freedom and love is on me as I fill my mind with thoughts of God and His promises. As I made room for God's love to take place in my life, I began to enjoy the other things in life that add to my happiness. My love for caring for myself and doing things I enjoy became my hobby. Each pay cycle, I treated myself to shopping, spas, dressed nicely, or just went to a restaurant and spoiled myself. Getting back into those simple hobbies was a life-changing part of me rediscovering myself.

Don't get me wrong, I loved being married and starting a family, but the time had come for me to enjoy once again what made me happy. Each day, I got a clearer sense of purpose in my life and loved me for me.

I love that beautiful young lady, Sheldine (me): her nationality, her personality, and everything she was and hopes to be. God's love did remove the fear, shame, and unforgiveness from my heart.

My year of release started in 2020. I had ongoing counseling classes, I talked about how I felt in all the sessions and, day by day, I overcame those emotions that lingered. After I experienced the mental abuse within my marriage and was suddenly on my own, I decided to take charge of my life. I realized that I always had a choice, but my choices before were made out of fear and shame and lack of self-confidence. Realizing all this, I started to be more appreciative and kinder to myself, trusting God fully.

I was offered the opportunity to be featured in a magazine and be a fashion model for a boutique. I enjoyed it all. My zeal to exercise also became a joy as I wanted to stay healthy and think constructively. To rediscover myself, I had to let go of the baggage of pain, stress and seek help if needed. I share my story, not for fame but to inspire others to tell their story, good or bad. Get help if you're in a bad situation or relationship. Get out and, most importantly, trust God in the process.

The best advice I will give people dealing with these situations is to find that love in God and truly love yourself. Do things that make you happy and give you peace of mind and joy. It is important for people to love themselves. After God, you have to love yourself truly! Only the love of God will allow you to have compassion for others as you move on in life. You will also have greater resilience to withstand the challenges in life. Accept who you are and believe that God loves you, as He created each of us uniquely.

1 CORINTHIANS 13:13, NIV:

And now these three remain: Faith, hope, and love. But the greatest of these is love.

Never Alone by Neisha Guy

I've had enough heartache

And I've had enough pain

And too many circumstances

Have left me out in the rain.

When I looked around me

When discouragement came

I fell down on my knees

Until I was whole again.

Here I stand before the world

Only because You were there.

Yeah, yeah, oh yeah.

Father, You lifted me

You lifted me higher.

And when I'm down you comfort me

Till I know I am stronger.

To be all you called me to be

I can be so much greater

Cause when I'm down you comfort me

Till I know that I'm stronger.

I've had enough Dog Days

And I've cried the most tears

And when the world could not hear me

I'm so glad that you did.

For everything, there's a time and a season

And change and I believe this one is mine

I believe it begins today.

Here I stand before the world only because

You were there, yeah, yeah, yeaheee...

Father, you lifted Me

You lifted Me higher

And when I'm down you comfort me

Till I know that I'm stronger

And it's because, oh it's because

You were there... for me, *for me*...

Father, you lifted Me, Father you lifted me

Yeah oh...oh!

Processing, Healing, and Reconnecting

"Healing yourself is connected with healing others."

- Yoko Ono

Healing does not happen instantly. It takes time to heal, be it to be healed from sickness or broken relationships/marriages.

I needed to have the right mindset to heal. I needed the time at my own pace to start healing. Some people are capable of self-healing. I needed to heal internally by releasing any past hurt or trauma I experienced before being married and while growing up in the care of my uncle.

I realized that I missed that embrace, attention, and love from my dad. While TV shows like *The Cosby Show* and *Family Matters* were funny, one part that stood out for me was the love in the family. I always imagined having a family, especially a husband, to fill that void of love.

My confidence in my abilities to fulfill my dreams of family was shattered as my dad wasn't there for me to have a healthy relationship with him. As I got older and experienced failed marriages, I began to question myself. *Wasn't I enough? Didn't I love enough, to the point my marriages failed?* My self-esteem plummeted and caused me to think I wasn't capable of keeping a marriage.

I wanted to be happy and owed it to myself to let go of the past. Once I heal, everything will fall into place. I believe one of the main things I had to deal with to heal stems from the void of not having a father figure in my younger days.

My dad migrated to the United States when I was five years old. I looked for love and comfort from anybody who presented themselves, which hurt me in the long run because the love I received wasn't genuine. The love I received came with conditions and restrictions.

I was timid and shy. I felt empty and anxious when I tried to speak my truth. Because I didn't face my problems and issues, I realized that my failed marriages had the same pattern and results. After my second marriage failed, I became determined to heal from my past. I went before God and asked Him to heal me since I couldn't do it by myself and I needed to release the pain and let go of the past.

> *"Time to open our baggage, because we can't board the plane with too many carry-ons."*
>
> *- Jason Wilson*

I encourage anyone dealing with failed marriages, relationships, or any bad situation to take time and heal. Healing will help you transition and discover what works and what doesn't work for you, making you better prepared next time. We need to pray and receive all that God has for us. Many of us have been hurt but too many of us have not been healed. A lack of healing will only result in more hurt and damage in your life.

In my healing, I treated myself kindly, gently, and in a supportive way similar to how I would support a loved one in need. I became completely confident in myself as I was healed through the love of God. I processed my pain with a constant prayer to God, as I felt useless, hurt, and a failure after my second divorce. Prayers surely helped and God being merciful to me assured me that it was only temporary pain.

Each day was different as time went by. Some days there were tears of joy while I wanted to shout out my praises to God for his provisions, be it financial, good health, or an enjoyable meal. I was finally able to manage my hurt by returning to God as my main source of love. This changed my life.

After my second divorce, I reconnected more with my dad. Even though he was sick, it was a joyous time for us as we reminisced. In the hospital, we bonded well and, each day, our love blossomed more and more. It was a joy for me to have the opportunity to care for him and be close to him as we openly expressed our love for each other.

These experiences with my dad helped me greatly in my healing process and helped my dad get better from diabetes. My dad became stronger each time we saw each other. Amidst the COVID 19 pandemic, we communicated every day on the phone and I thanked God for the opportunity to reconnect with my Dad.

My network of friends and co-authors grew. Despite the COVID 19 pandemic, I participated in numerous virtual projects and activities. I was motivated to be resilient and strong. I needed to be aligned with the right people to help me keep my head above water.

My church ministry, the network of young entrepreneurs and co-authors, and my small circle of trusted friends were all sent by God to steer me in the right direction and help me make it through the journey.

When my story was featured in the book *Evolution Effect*, the memory electrified me. Seeing my picture and title was a moment to celebrate. I loved my glow and I felt good blossoming like a flower.

I thought back on the day my life came to a screeching halt. I felt lonely and I was immensely hurt when my daughter was separated from me again while I lived with my then-husband. Those were indeed sad days, but I believed God had a bigger plan for us. My daughter was able to return to her country of birth and bond with her biological dad whom she had yearned for many years.

While I learned to adjust to my new environment, my daughter processed her healing in a different country with her dad. At first, it was hard for both of us. I felt angry about my decision and questioned God. However, each time, He wrapped me in His arms and comforted me, provided for me, and made all that seemed impossible possible!

At that time, I also became more connected to God. I learned more of His word which gave me comfort. Following His guidance through scriptures, God prompted me to continue to write more and, each day, I smiled more and felt better.

I shared God's word and the encouragement I received with my daughter and with people who struggle in a bad situation. I prayed each day (and still do). My life became better because I felt better. I would chuckle to myself in amazement with my progress.

Thank you, God, my Healer, and my Everything!

My daughter and I eventually reconnected. We embraced, kissed, and cried together for joy. I could not stop praising God and I knew I needed Him more.

Start your journey of processing, healing, and reconnecting.

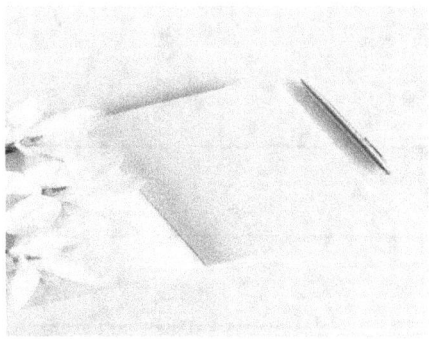

YOUR THOUGHTS

What hurt, pain, trauma, disappointment, and regret are you holding on to?

Pain

_____

_____

_____

_____

_____

_____

Trauma

_____

_____

_____

_____

_____

_____

Disappointment

_____

_____

_____

_____

_____

_____

Regret

_____

_____

_____

_____

_____

In order for you to truly move forward in your life, you must forgive. Forgive the person who caused you pain, but above all, forgive yourself.

I Forgive MYSELF for

_____

_____

_____

_____

_____

_____

I Forgive MYSELF for

_____

_____

_____

_____

_____

I Forgive MYSELF for

_____

_____

_____

_____

_____

_____

I Forgive MYSELF for

Processing, Healing, and Reconnecting

Breathe and Exhale

My favorite song to start the day was, and still is, *I am crossing over*. I have grown to love the song after a friend and co-author shared it on her page on Facebook. It resonated with my heart and spirit. I sing it every morning. I sing to God to help me with my *crossovers*, for I know He has a bigger plan for my life.

Today, I am brimming with energy and overflowing with joy. I advise you to *breathe and exhale*. Breathing properly decreases stress, pain, and anxiety. When you breathe in, air enters your lungs, and oxygen from the air moves from your lungs to your blood. It is important to breathe and exhale!

In my situation, breathing helps me to ease the strain on my heart when I am stressed and confused. Breathing exercises help clear my mind of negativity as I try to think of solutions to my problems. It purifies, releases, and soothes different parts of my body when I am hurt and extremely overwhelmed.

In marital disagreements, I found it hard to express myself well. The frustration I felt caused my heart to beat rapidly. When nervous, I would shake and tremble a lot. Sometimes, negative criticisms about my family and me would trigger a chain of stress reactions, making me cry and break down.

Sometimes, we feel that our situation is the worst in life until we listen to another person's story that makes our jaw drop in astonishment. We can all learn and grow from each other's stories.

In a conference at church, a married couple shared their story about how a massive brain stem stroke almost killed the wife. I listened closely as they recounted different stages and struggles they had to overcome. They overcame so much because they did not give up their hope and trust in God. Hope, and not just any hope, but hope and trust in God gave them strength to overcome that much. This story has helped millions of people around the world. I cried throughout that conference. I hope that my story will help others heal too.

My favorite affirmations are:

- **I am the strongest woman I know. I have patience. I am my own rescue.**

- **I am willing to see things differently. I am willing to forgive myself.**

- **I see my current circumstances as opportunities to grow.**

- **I release the past and trust that everything is happening for my greatest good.**

- **Everything I am going through is making me a stronger, wiser, and more compassionate person.**

It is important to say affirmations every day and to take a moment to breathe and exhale. I do this every morning when I wake up and at night right before I go to bed. I sit in complete quietness and allow that peace of God to come over me and give me calmness in the midst of all the chaos and confusion.

Have you ever watched any movies that showed the strict and militant sergeant in the army or boot camp? Well, my marriage was somewhat like that after some months of living together. It was like you had to always be on your P's and Q's and walk on eggshells.

At home, movies were screened. If it didn't say Jesus, it was deemed a bad movie, and the children and I couldn't watch it. In a moment of rage, the TVs were taken down and placed in boxes. I reverted to using my phone to view movies.

A simple thing as a sneeze and replying *bless you* was a big upset. *How dare you say bless you? Are you God?* That bothered me but I dared not try to explain. My inner voice wanted to say it was something that I was used to saying as a child. To argue that point or anything, for the most part, I was summoned in the bedroom for a *meeting* and then I knew something was wrong.

My heart raced; anxiety and nerves would kick in all at once. All this was to hear his explanation. To say *Merry Christmas, Happy New Year, or Happy Birthday* was also not allowed. I was confused, just as my children were because this was not the person I married.

Sometimes as we heard the sound of the music from his phone in the corridor. It made us aware that the *sergeant*, my then-husband was approaching our apartment. We scampered to fix everything right and that was of great stress and anxiety, but my technique worked. I took deep breaths and allowed the calmness to flow.

Then there was the click of the doorknob. We prepared to greet him, while his eyes were fixed on everything, we were mindful of how we expressed ourselves.

Things shifted from bad to worse. At that point, my daughter, wanting some free time like any other teenager, was also faced with her challenges. This eventually led to him asking her to leave the home, coming out of the many constant back and forth arguments. She was told to comb her hair a certain way, couldn't wear earrings, and sometimes she and my son had to kneel with their hands up as punishment. That not being enough, they were physically abused with a belt while I was not there.

I tolerated this for months while I worked, posted my pictures on Facebook, and pretended to live a normal happy life. I was ashamed to tell anyone of my situation and feared my marriage would end. All this was the beginning of my stress but I was still in denial. I thought he was doing all this because he loved me. Day by day, with constant prayers to God for help and to direct me to the right persons to seek help, I made it through. I continued to use my technique to breathe and exhale.

My son was there with me after my daughter left. I wanted to give him all my love and support as he missed his sister. However, to openly express my love to him with a hug or just verbalizing it, sometimes came with some scrutiny from my husband. A sharp look from his eyes like I did something wrong or, as he would have said, *the way you're loving your son*, suggesting I was loving or thinking of my ex-husband and son's father.

To just appear home from work without an announcement would have led to an argument. Even though we didn't have a car, he would travel every night to pick me up. Some of my work colleagues saw it as *love*, but I knew it wasn't as I was not happy but went with the flow. Sometimes I got a lot of tension at work as he approached my workplace. I had to check how I communicated with my work colleagues: a loud laugh or to look at someone may appear too suggestive to him. As I recalled one day, I planned not to announce I was headed home and wanted to be spontaneous and just showed up and surprised him. That didn't go well at all. I was so confused but, again, expressing my truth caused much anxiety and stress. I kept my cool, breathed, and exhaled.

My son and I were both tense and I realized it started to affect him in school, not his grades but he was timid about expressing and participating in some classes. He started being inattentive. Things he usually did in school were no longer happening and the teachers called me in. At that moment, I knew I needed a third-party intervention.

I prayed about it and reached out to one of my church ministers in Trinidad. We discussed everything and she advised counseling and continued prayers to God for peace and restoration. I was not only looking to help myself and my son, but I wanted to help my then-husband, in my second marriage, to be a better and loving husband.

In a very soft tone, trying to be very brave while my heart raced, I was able to convince him to go to counseling. Our sessions were great at first but after a few sessions, he didn't want to return after being told of his wrongdoings. He had the perfect answer: *why tell your problems to a man (the marriage counselor)? Is he God?* (Déjà vu, anyone?) He decided he was not going back.

Back at square one, I went before God again and cried my heart out for help as I knew more help, more prayers, and more support were needed. I feared leaving and what my family and friends might think of me having another failed marriage. I had constant headaches.

I remembered he told me I needed to leave the apartment and he had packed my things. He said things like, *You will never get a cheap rent like this apartment.*

My thoughts were all over the place:

Where would I stay?

Should I tell anyone else?

Was there something wrong with me?

Breathe, Sheldine, breathe!

I continued attending my counseling at church alone, still trying to find out if I was the one who needed the personal help (again thinking I had a problem). After those sessions, I knew for a fact that the only thing I needed was to get out of my marriage. That time I opened up to my close families and friends. Thanks to God, the support was there. Things didn't change in my marriage but it was comforting to know that I had support other than God. That in itself eased my stress.

There were so many other events and occurrences that took place as our marriage was ending that, mentally, I was a wreck! The mental and psychological abuse was killing me inside. He told me not to do anything in the home, like washing, cooking, etc., but I continued.

There was a day I clearly remember him repeating that I should not make the bed. Being filled with fear, I complied. To my surprise, he recorded a video of himself with a sound warning and sent it to my phone, saying how I allowed the devil to overtake me and what would happen if it *ever* happened again. There were constant messages on my phone thereon even though we lived in the same apartment.

More rules and restrictions were set in the apartment and I observed more changes daily like things of sentimental value missing from the home. I inquired about some of the missing things and was told that those were materialistic things and he had sold them. Believe it or not, one of those *materialistic* things was his wedding ring!

In my mind, again, I was like huh? Is he really a man of God? Really? Amid all the rules and tension, in the same breath, he would summon me to the bedroom for sex. I referred to it as just sex since it didn't feel like the love between a married couple.

One night I felt so hurt, cheap and useless, but I did what I had to do as a wife after being told *you need to be submissive to your husband; it's written in the Bible*. At the time, my son was on his summer vacation so I was there alone trying to figure out all this and my next move. Breathe, Sheldine, breathe and exhale!

I knew my then-husband to be a strong believer in God, but these things troubled me and I tapped into his family to find out if maybe he had any past hurt or situations. My inquiry was to no avail. I was determined to get help after that. After more counseling sessions with my minister, I realized this was control and not love. His asking me to leave his apartment really would work for my good.

So when he came home one day and gave me a date to leave by, I used that as my fixed point in moving on. My freedom and torture were soon going to be over, even though I knew it would be hard on me. At that moment, I said *thank you, Lord*. I needed to move on to my new life. I was now ready to breathe, but with the newness, freshness, and sweetness of life. I knew God was making way for me. Day by day, I stopped being hard on myself and my support team increased.

I finally got the courage and strength and was able to move out. Lord knows it wasn't an easy move. Actually, it was HARD! I slept like a baby that night, though.

The next morning, my phone pinged as a video message came in from my then-husband. He expressed that our marriage was not real as *he got a revelation from God* to go back to his ex-wife since she was alive and I should do the same too. I was not surprised by that because, by that time, I was used to all his religious beliefs and theories. I knew I had nothing to hold onto by holding onto him and I was already out of the apartment, trusting God for healing, peace, and help.

Today, my hope is to encourage persons dealing with marital problems, physical or mental abuse, or separation to trust God in the process and to have a personal relationship with Jesus. I entrusted my ex-husband in almost everything, more than I trusted God.

I believed this destroyed me; I know it separated me from my daughter, deepening my unhappiness.

My ex-husband tried to change me to his ways and religious beliefs rather than allow God to change me. I was not having the relationship with God that I should have had: Satan stepped in instead. To those who don't know Jesus as your personal Lord and Savior, get to know Him and seek help. Learn to forgive as we all have our own wrongdoings and are not perfect. No one is perfect but God.

Breathe and exhale, just like I did, and overcome your hurt and pain. I did and you can too. Breathing and exhaling allowed me to be calm, listen, and not speak when the other voice is louder than mine.

Breathe and Exhale

Patience and Peace

Patience and Peace:

"One minute of patience, ten years of peace."

- Greek Proverb

"Patience is not the ability to wait, but the ability to keep a good attitude while waiting."

-Joyce Meyer

"Patience": *The capacity to accept or tolerate delay, trouble, or suffering without getting angry or upset*[1].

"Peace": *Is a stress-free state of security and calmness that comes when there's no fighting or war, everything coexisting in perfect harmony and freedom*[2].

Patience is very important while you wait because being impatient will not make God move any faster. Many times, we want a *quick fix* in our situations. I am guilty too and would rather get over my hurt and trust issues as quickly as possible. Now, I know that God

---

[1] "PATIENCE." *Lexico.Com*, Lexico Dictionaries, https://www.lexico.com/en/definition/patience. Accessed 13 May 2021.

[2] "Peace - Dictionary Definition." Vocabulary.Com, https://www.vocabulary.com/dictionary/peace. Accessed 13 June 2021.

was moving and speaking to me through the process. God was preparing me as He was putting things in place for me.

Confused and pained? I was indeed! There are many other words I can use to describe my recent divorce. It was not an easy experience for my children or me. Nevertheless, I know I am a strong woman and the divorce helped me grow.

Can you imagine you and your family migrating to a new country in the hope of betterment, care, and love, only to have everything change in a matter of a few months? Instead of your lives changing over a period of time, your lives change OVERNIGHT. It was like all my expectations and dreams were smashed!

This journey has not been easy and, if you've experienced leaving your country of birth or a country you once called home to a new environment, I bet you can relate. After being comfortable, managing my affairs, working, and having my friends and family's help and support, I found myself in a place where minimal support was available. It was hard!

What was I going to do? Where was I going to live? How would I manage the rent and expenses all by myself? These questions brought *fear* to my heart. I know for a fact that I didn't have all the answers and, at that point, only God and His mercy could help me out.

As I was taught in church, *fear is the opposite of faith* and *faith without works is dead*. I started to work even harder. Long hours in the office to get the extra overtime money to cover my day-to-day expenses, rent, food, and I still tried to save. This was very hard on my body, physically and mentally; I had a nervous breakdown and was sick for a while. Stress is not easy.

I recovered with medication, continued prayers to God, and support from those who knew what I was going through. This was a period of tremendous personal growth. Even though they were small steps, they counted!

These lessons helped me grow and brought peace of mind. I did some short courses to enhance myself for the job market and make a quick turnover in my finances. I also started investing in the costume jewelry business and did some small fashion modeling for boutiques. Things turned around slowly, but every time I reflected on my experience, it pushed me to do more.

I was not going to give up and never will. In all this, I saw all I was capable of doing on my own and gradually turned things around. All my activities allowed me to focus ahead and the sky was the limit for me. Thank you Jesus for your faithfulness! I am proud of the fact that I never let go of His presence while the devil tried to test my patience. I came out victorious with the peace and love of God upon me.

Sometimes, our patience and peace can be tested by our very own children. My children are my everything after God. Everything I do is for them: my work, desire to live healthily, care, and concern. When my teen daughter acted out and was rebellious because she was no longer with me, all my patience was tested. Fear and anxiety set within.

I was fearful for her physical safety, fearful about her being able to make wise choices and, most of all, fearful that she wouldn't stay faithful to God. I had to stay prayed up and renew my commitment to pray faithfully for her and my son. I knew in the absence of my physical presence, my only support was a prayer to God for His covering and protection over my daughter's life. Each day, I prayed Ephesians 6:1-3 over her life.

While I was at my previous job, my patience and peace were tested. A situation occurred and took me right back to memory lane. I remembered being shouted at, taken advantage of, and I just wanted to scream. My then manager abused her power and made changes that made her feel good, while she hurt me and another staff member. (Had I not known God...Oh boy!)

I was tempted to react but I knew that reacting would only bring me temporary satisfaction and, ultimately, destroy my peace. That day, choking back tears, I tried to be observant when I became agitated by her actions. I composed myself, used my breathing and exhaling technique, and even uttered a prayer right there. I believed she heard me and raised her voice again in anger: *Are you speaking to me?*

As I finished my prayer, I attempted to respond thoughtfully rather than react. I said very firmly and in a strong tone:

> "Ma'am, I am not speaking to you. When you can, control your emotions; it's awesome!"

I believe I did a rather good job of practicing patience. Even though that was her overall attitude, I ignored her and prayed for her to get better. I went before God again and asked that He continue to direct my path as I had to take a new step of faith to grow further and face my new adventures.

Sometimes, it takes a bad situation to remind or show you that you deserve better and that better exist! Today, I am prepared to move to my new place and a new job with great and better expectations for myself and my family. Sometimes growth requires a new company, new locations, and a new mindset.

Some advice I will share with you if your patience and peace are being tested:

Pray and allow yourself to be still. Remember that once you are aligned with God, all the pieces of the puzzle will fall into place at the right time.

Listen and keep your silence. Give others time to say what they need to say and have them repeat it to verify that you understood correctly. This might seem like a no-brainer, but most people aren't as good at listening as they think they are. Active listening is a skill that takes time and practice to develop.

Try to stay calm. I know this is very hard for some as it was for me. When my patience gets tested, I try to look ahead and think because doing something in anger will hurt us sooner than we think. As the saying goes, haste makes waste.

Every one of us has a point of reference by which we can testify about the goodness of God in our lives. My faith in God has grown stronger and deeper now than before when I was not a believer in God and I was so confused. I went through relationship breakups and felt worthless, helpless, and dependent on others for assistance.

My daily prayer to God was for patience. I needed to be patient as I raised my children. I needed to be patient at work dealing with different personalities and delivering my daily tasks. Time, patience, and trust in God really changed me as I strongly believe that what is to come is blessed and worth waiting for.

My prayer:

Father God, I am reinvigorated in my faith and I hunger each day for God's love in my life. Continue to hold my hands and keep my heart always for you.

I declare the purpose of my life and declare you are my source of love. I pray all the readers accept you in their lives, in Jesus's name. Amen.

Patience and Peace

Great Momentum

"I can't change the direction of the wind, but I can adjust my sails to always reach my destination."

- Jimmy Dean

Life is beautiful.

Life is what you make it.

I remember the day I was asked if I wanted to write a book. At first, I smiled at the thought because I never seriously thought of becoming an author. I have always imagined myself as a fashion model.

I was nervous but decided to put pen to paper. I began to write by recalling some events in my life. Every day I wrote a chapter. Each chapter I wrote was a therapeutic experience.

Recounting my past experiences and putting them down on paper ushered the beginning of my healing process. In both of my previous marriages, I experienced verbal and physical abuse which greatly affected my mental and physical health. It was painful to be criticized because of one's nationality. The discrimination angered me. I vowed not to trust and love a man with a different nationality from mine.

Sometimes the words came easy. Sometimes my mind would sputter and freeze. Regardless of the disruptions and distractions, I kept at it and I felt more at ease as time went by and journaling became a habit. God's helping hand was there to guide and comfort me. My writing cushioned and strengthened me to keep moving on the path of healing. Being as motivated and determined as ever after my first published chapter, I became more ready and confident in telling my story.

No more secrets. No more control. No more fake smiles to hide the pain.

As I wrote, I remembered my wedding day: the joy, the music, the people, and the beautiful setting. What a beautiful day and moment it was. *A great momentum*, I thought and smiled. Our vows were based on love for each other; our dance and interaction with each other were great!

That day we laughed hard! I recalled how I tried to put the ring on his finger during the ceremony and it was not going on! We had to apply soap and water before it went on. That was so funny then. We chuckled even as we looked at the video months later.

Our pictures came out wonderful and I looked like a princess and he looked like a prince.

Congrats to the beautiful couple! Let's see the diamond on her finger!

Some of the guests were anxious to view it and I showed it off with a smile. While I hoped to live happily ever after, life events happened and I'm now divorced.

We all experience love in some form and experience some heartbreak too. I believe that all my challenges, failures, and happy times helped me to become the person I am today. I can say it isn't an easy process: I needed patience, kindness, and trust in God while allowing the process of healing to take place.

I have always been an emotional person. I cried and there were some days I broke down and felt like a failure again. I went before God, sometimes even while in my bathroom, and cried out to him to increase my faith in Him and help me along the way. Everything happens for a reason and there is a purpose for everything although we often don't know what it is at the time.

Now don't get me wrong, marriage is beautiful. We had happy times as a family and I'm grateful to God for all the good and bad times. But the circumstances and events that transpired in our marriage led to divorce.

I had to speak up and face my fears and let go as I didn't see any change happening if I stayed. Months passed and, over the course of two years, I started to find myself again. I learned to trust God first and my instincts second, for there was more for me to attain in life. Some see me today and say:

You're doing well. You look well!

They don't know the journey it took me to reach this point of *wellness*.

Life is not all about material things. While I'm convinced material things can contribute to one's happiness, I know that peace of mind, a good spiritual side, and a relationship with God are important. I had to learn to make time to spend quality time reading and studying God's word and stop allowing others to control my life or emotions.

I also worked on bettering myself in different aspects. An opportunity to write a chapter was given to me in the book *Love Changed Me*. My journey continues day by day and, each day, I noticed my potential and strengths. My life is destined for greatness.

Having awesome support from friends and family—the kindness and most authentic love I have received—throughout this journey keeps me humbled. Trust me, I could not have done it all on my own.

They encouraged me whenever I failed and wanted to give up. Someone is always praying for me. It is like God set up all these persons and opportunities for me.

I recall one day feeling so overwhelmed with all my finances and unsure which direction to go. My phone rang and it was a call from my church requesting to pray for me if I needed prayer. That was so timely and I know that God is always with me. I am becoming something new in Christ Jesus.

To everyone reading this book, let your challenges be your breakthrough to greatness. Let it be your testimony that will not only heal you but others as well. Always trust God in the process of your life.

Affirmations:

- **Today we are affirming your GREAT MOMENTUM to move forward!**

- **Today is the day to become renewed and affirm the life of success and freedom!**

YOUR THOUGHTS

Today I give myself permission to:

_____

_____

_____

_____

_____

_____

_____

I give myself permission to honor my mind, body, soul, and spirit by:

_____

_____

_____

_____

_____

I will no longer allow people to dictate my feelings or experiences of:

_____

_____

_____

_____

_____

I give myself permission to no longer:

_____

_____

_____

_____

_____

I give myself permission to be:

_____

_____

_____

_____

_____

_____ every day.

Give yourself permission to love on you EVERY DAY!

Great Momentum

Growth, New Adventures, and Being Intentional

"Without continual growth and progress, such words as improvement, achievement, and success have no meaning."

-Benjamin Franklin

By facing and overcoming many challenges and adversities, I learned more about myself and my self-worth. I realized that I am responsible for the outcome of my relationships and my life. I began to take the opportunity to develop and reinvent myself and focus on what truly matters. My standards and expectations for myself became a reflection of my newfound self-respect and the power to take hold of my life.

As my maturity, sensibility, and insight grew on how to build better relationships with my family and children, I began to make sense of taking responsibility and reaping the benefits from a loving and authentic relationship. There is so much to receive when you focus on what is good and what can be made better in the face of negativity and adversities. I became more attuned to the *soft* language of communication. I became mindful of the tone of my voice and overall body language. I wanted my loved ones to feel my love and also to receive their love.

I no longer force things. Forcing things is stressful and stress only adds to the pressure and feelings of emptiness, helplessness, and fearfulness common after broken relationships. I witnessed my relatives and friends suffer from stress and even mourned their passing from illness brought on from too much unmanaged stress. Because of this awareness, I resolved to become healthy by consistently strengthening my mind and body with exercise. I wanted to be physically fit to help steer and stabilize my mind and strength to face and overcome whatever curveballs life throws at me.

My second divorce ignited the sparks of change and ultimately inspired me to unlearn what is no longer working for me and to learn what I needed to do and act on my values. I needed to unlearn my long-held outlook on anger and survival. I needed to learn to release my pain and anger. I needed to forgive so I could live with the pain and reap the wisdom from the lessons without hurting myself or anyone anymore.

It is one thing to say *I have forgiven*. It another thing to feel the peace of having truly forgiven when moral tradition and principles dictate for us to forgive, but the heart has been shattered and is trying to protect itself by holding onto the anger. Holding onto anger made me want to lash out at my ex-husband, even though he was asking for forgiveness. I interpreted his request to mean I would no longer blame him and hold him accountable for his shortcomings and the pain and suffering he caused me.

A friend and spiritual sister advised me to say *thank you* and to genuinely wish him well; to truly feel in my heart that I want to forgive him. To do this, I needed to let go of the past and stop judging him. I knew I needed to forgive him and myself to help my heart heal and be ready to love and receive love again. When I am ready to love and receive love again, I will begin to feel the peace and lightness of true forgiveness.

I needed to grow because I wanted to realize my dreams and potential as a person, as a mother, as a single parent, and in everything else that I participated in. I wanted to develop my skills so that I could provide financially for my children. Some days I felt overwhelmed after a long day at work, but I never gave up. Every day, I ask God to help me love my neighbor as I love myself by being considerate and positive.

My intention is to inspire people and offer encouragement amid hardships and failures. My hard life made me want to become a better person for myself and others. My hard life and struggles brought out the best in me instead of defeating what is good and pure in me as intended by God with His sufficient grace.

> *"If you don't go after what you want, you'll never have it.*
>
> *If you don't ask, the answer is always no.*
>
> *If you don't step forward, you're always in the same place."*
>
> *-Nora Roberts*

To be intentional means having a clear purpose in life. It means taking action based on the clarity and certainty of your thoughts, the purity of your values, and the spirit of compassion.

My growth plan was and is foremost in my mind. I want to live my life to the fullest. With God's love and guidance, what was impossible for me as a human being became possible and produced full of strength and hope. My faith in God and a solid support system helped me heal and grow.

I took some serious time to learn from my mistakes, take responsibility, forgive myself, and heal. My priorities became focused on myself, my children, and God's love with guidance. Despite the pain of my divorce, I became intentional in serving God for God said (1 John 1:9, NIV): *"If we confess our sins, he is faithful and just and will forgive us our sins and purify us from all unrighteousness."*

In 2020, the entire world was turned upside-down. Masks replaced smiles. There were no more hugs and there was less human interaction. Many families lost their loved ones and many people lost their jobs. It was hard for everybody.

2020 became a time for self-reflection and to rediscover the most important things in life. During this time, I stepped into faith and invested in a website as a means to start my business, whether in books or clothing. It was also like a form of therapy for me.

The year 2020 was the time when I became purposeful with my healing. I grew my circle with positive people to learn and grow from as well as celebrate life with. Constant compliments on my growth from one of my mentors/friends encouraged me to press on. I was determined to be the best version of myself. God has truly blessed me with an awesome support team.

As I remember in my first podcast, I was so nervous when I told my story, but as time went on, I became more at ease. The more I stepped out in faith the more I felt supported. Everything was natural. I have *it* in me!

> *"It was beautiful, the way she held herself with such grace, such poise, such dignity.*
>
> **One wouldn't have ever guessed that behind that fair expression, kind smile, and compassionate face, there was a scarred fragile heart and a torn-up soul, yearning for a place to feel safe and loved."**
>
> *- Angelina Zoe*

With God's guidance and direction, I set new goals for myself. My mindset changed to being responsible for my growth and I wanted to work for everything: first for God as He has done so much for me.

God blesses our faithfulness. I know by faith my financial situation will change, not for the worse but the better, as that is now my focus. My goals are to save to support my children, college, special activities, and something for retirement. My goal is also to have a better relationship with my children, friends, and family. Spending quality time with them, either at home, on my days off, or on a vacation is a high priority for me. Going through these situations, I was also able to evaluate my friends. Not trying to be judgmental, but I needed to have friends that would support and encourage me in this chapter of my life. So do you!

I needed a fun goal, yes, more room for laughter, travel, and to prioritize the enjoyment of my new life. After being in a tense relationship, I wanted the fun of freedom of speech, expression, and love. Owning my own home is also my priority to just enjoy my peace in my own space. That to me gives a sense of pride and accomplishment for myself and my children. Having moved from different countries and towns, I need stability. My prayer to God is to help me set these goals and commit to making them a reality.

The only effective way to grow is through prayers to God. We need to ask God to help and direct us through this process. In receiving His direction, we need to have the discipline to work diligently on our goals to better our lives and fulfill the dreams He has placed in our hearts. If we encounter being divorced, hurt in relationships, or any setbacks or challenges in life, just trust in God.

When the love of God starts to flow through our activities, everything becomes light! Had I not known and experienced the love of God, I believe I would still be suffering to get past my hurt. This suffering causes much damage to not only yourself but to your children and family.

Change is also a great way to measure the true strength of your growth. While some people find it hard to adapt to change, I did too, it's worth it. My most recent big change was relocating to another state. This decision came after much deliberation: a fresh start, a new start, and a new job.

Many days I had headaches and sleepless nights, but I had to remind myself of the God I serve. God is in control and, as long as He is, all is and will be well even when fear tries to overpower me.

"Life's challenges are not supposed to paralyze you, they're supposed to help you discover who you are."

- Bernice Johnson Reagon

It is important to grow through your journey: I grew through my divorce, work challenges, and everyday ups and downs. In every step or situation, you come out a winner. Challenges are growth opportunities and, with good self-control, you will soon find yourself at the next level.

Congratulations, you are growing! All praise be to God!

"We can't become what we need to be by remaining what we are."

- Oprah Winfrey

Growth, New Adventures, and Being Intentional

YOUR THOUGHTS

Describe an adversity you overcame. How were you able to move forward?

_____

_____

_____

_____

_____

_____

_____

What is an expectation you have of a partner? What are your non-negotiables?

_____

_____

_____

_____

_____

What advice would you give to a person struggling with communication in their relationships?

_____

_____

_____

_____

_____

_____

You have to be intentional about your growth, your life, and your success. How are you being intentional with setting up your day?

_____

_____

_____

_____

Ask yourself, are you satisfied with your life in these areas: career, personal, relational, and financial?

If yes, move on to the next question. If no, why?

_____

_____

_____

_____

_____

In what areas do you find yourself striving?

_____

_____

_____

_____

_____

Describe your idea of success?

_____

_____

_____

_____

_____

_____

What is holding you back from taking the leap? Be specific; what are your fears? What are you passionate about?

_____

_____

_____

_____

_____

_____

Growth, New Adventures, and Being Intentional

Finally Loving On Me

I started to use the #Loveonme on most of my social media accounts, which constantly reminded me I needed to love myself more. I also realized how much I missed in my life as I constantly loved people more than myself. Being a people pleaser, trying to love myself first was challenging. The #Loveonme became my mantra which made the necessary personal changes and adjustments easier.

Whenever and wherever I share my story, I do so to inspire others to share their own stories, good or bad, always encouraging them to reach out for help and to keep on trusting and hoping in God.

Self-introspection is important to one's growth. I needed to identify my problem. I needed to take stock of where I was stuck in life, in my relationships, and in any place where I might be going through the motions without any idea if a situation or relationship is aligned with my values. In my reflections, I realized I needed to do something to help myself become better.

Before I got married, self-care was a priority. It all changed when I married my second husband whose religious beliefs clashed with that kind of lifestyle. I realized that if I had to rediscover myself, I needed to get in touch with who I was and what I did to express self-love.

I loved being married and having a family, but to be present for my family, I needed to take care of myself first. Having a clear purpose in life and staying true to my values, I fell more in love with the beautiful Sheldine: her nationality, personality, and everything she was and will become.

I started my counseling classes. I talked about my feelings and my state of mind. By being honest and acknowledging my wide spectrum of human emotions, I was able to deal with my unresolved issues. I was also offered to be featured in a magazine. I modeled for a boutique which I extremely enjoyed. I looked forward to exercising and keeping fit because I wanted to stay in good health and work on my dreams.

I dropped my baggage and the things that were holding me back, the pain. I sought help. I knew I needed help.

I challenge you to have and develop your personal relationship with God. Prove to the world that the love of God is on you. Become that love for God first and ALL your challenges and adversities in life will pass with ease. This love, God's love, will be unlike any other. **Love On Me**, God!

"Remember God doesn't want us to know the future; He wants us to know Him."

- Stormie Omartian

Daily Mantras

- I surrender my worries to God.

- I release my past and forgive myself.

- Things will always work out in my favor through God.

Meet the Author

Sheldine Gordon is a 2X Author of books *The Evolution Effect* and *Love On Me*. She is a very humble woman of God and an overcomer of many circumstances.

Having a great story of her past and present ingrained in her the need to share and motivate people dealing with failed relationships, migration, and family struggles. The hope of sharing the beauty of life birthed by challenges and unforeseen circumstances was her desire to create this book project.

Connect with Sheldine Gordon via:

Website: sheldinegordon.com

Facebook: fb.com/sheldine.gordon

Instagram: instagram.com/sheldine.gordon

We would love to hear your perspective. Stay in touch at loveonmebook.com and don't forget to leave a review on Amazon and Goodreads.

Life is all about experiences and perspectives.

We asked powerful, game-changing women to share their views.

LOVE ON ME

Meet the Author

Featured Guest Contributors:

Simone N. Bharath

Dr. Deena Brown

Neisha Guy

Noreen N. Henry

Monica Reed

Vernae Taylor

Simone N. Bharath

During the first four years of my career, I was robbed twice at gunpoint. A few years later, sheer will, determination, and tenacity of just wanting to succeed after a traumatizing experience is what helped me to move forward.

My grandfather's words *a quitter never wins, and a winner never quits* helped me stay focused. By 2010, I was an educator alongside international educators for the brand *Ashtae*. These challenges showed the main lifeline was God in business first beyond everything.

Having a partner, whether personal or professional, I've set high standards of honesty and transparency which go hand in hand. Being paired with the right partner and evenly yoked is the key ingredient for a formidable, successful relationship and continued communication. My non-negotiable would be my brand and having God at the helm of business and relationships.

For a person struggling with communication in their relationship(s), I would advise them that the greatest teacher of communication in relationships is God. Following instructions and being obedient to God's instructions are the main keys for success if you find yourself struggling in your relationship. Also, one needs to be able to identify the strong points and weaknesses in their relationship(s) to move forward. Therefore, having God as the center of your relationship makes communication and transitioning easier.

Simone N. Bharath, of Trinidad and Tobago, is the CEO and Founder of Exousia Beauty Spa and Salon for the past 21 years. Simone is the founder of Unmasked Women's Empowerment, which uses Exousia as the tool to reach out to hurting women in our society, helping them remove their masks step by step.

She is also a distributor of an international product line, *Ashtae Multicultural Product*, based in North Carolina, U.S. She is a mentor to various schools around the country and a speaker in many small and startup companies. She has been featured in local newspapers and television.

Connect with Simone N. Bharath:

Instagram: instagram.com/exousiabeautyspa

Facebook: fb.com/simone.bharath

Meet the Author

Dr. Deena Brown

Everything I've done in my career is to inspire, empower, and transform lives. It has looked different throughout my life: from the classroom and corporate boardrooms to stages around the world.

Today it's about building a strategy for women who want to transform their lives—the go-to leaders. If everyone goes to YOU when things go wrong, who do YOU call? Well, now you can call me. I've been there, trapped by the ideas everyone else told me would fit my life. I'll take your moments of chaos and indecision and create clarity around your ideas and products.

Learning to love me *on purpose with purpose* was the greatest adversity I have overcome. Once I learned how to put myself first and check in with *me*, I have been able to serve from my overflow while I sip on my own genius.

My expectation of my partner is to honor and respect me with my flaws and in my fabulosity. Mean people are non-negotiable for me. I can work around many attitudes and behaviors but I will not tolerate mean people.

For persons struggling with communication in their relationships, I would advise them to check their temperature before beginning to communicate with those they love. If you are feeling *heated*, cool down before sharing your thoughts. Your words are like toothpaste and once they are out, they cannot be put back inside the tube.

Dr. Deena Brown has been working in Organizational Development, Executive Coaching, Organizational Change & Transformation, and Leadership Development for over 20 years. After identifying a significant deficit of women in key leadership roles, Dr. Brown founded The Leadhershift Movement® and created The Leadhershift Incubator, a robust community where women develop UNSHAKABLE CLARITY, UNDENIABLE CONFIDENCE, AND UNSTOPPABLE CONSISTENCY that will give them the competitive advantage to EXCEL in LIFE and BUSINESS. Today, it's about building a strategy for women who want to transform their lives—the go-to leaders.

Dr. Brown is:

- the C.E.O. of Her Executive Presence, LLC., an executive coaching company for female executives.

- host of the podcast Her Executive Presence.

- co-host of a weekly talk show "Interludes" on Srishti T.V.

- an international best-selling author.

Dr. Deena Brown is currently researching the intersectionality of imposter syndrome with race, class, and trauma amongst African American women and other minority ethnic groups. She holds a Ph.D. from the University of Southern Mississippi in Educational Leadership and Research; M.A. in Education from Old Dominion University; and a B.A. in Economics from San Diego State University.

Connect with Dr. Deena Brown:

Website: leadhershiftmovement.com

Instagram: instagram.com/drdeenaspeaks

Facebook: fb.com/DrDeenaCBrown

Twitter: twitter.com/drdeenaspeaks

LinkedIn: linkedin.com/in/drdeenacbrown

Neisha Guy

I became pregnant for the first time at age 28. I was very ill and hospitalized for about two months. Pre-eclampsia was threatening the life of the baby and I.

Fourteen days before the baby's due date, the doctor threw me out of the hospital. I went back on the due date only to find out that my baby had died. They left him in me for close to four days. They waited for me to die.

I am still recovering both physically and mentally. Being weak, not able to move, I was determined to walk again, started to exercise, and continued to sing. Being on autopilot for over three years, I started to love myself again even though I looked and felt differently. God's intervention, my love for music, and singing truly helped me.

I am an independent woman. I refuse to be with a man with less drive, passion, ambition, or energy than

I. After putting a man together and rubbing him with gold for other women to have him, I do not want a fixer-upper. Give me a man who knows he is a King and I am his Queen. Another non-negotiable of mine is smoking. No smoking allowed.

The advice I would give to a person struggling with communication in his or her relationship is to practice patience. There's a thin line between love and devotion. Devotion can hurt, especially when both partners are not devoted. Your efforts to build in communication will be in vain.

However, if both parties are truly willing to build an understanding of their **love language and dark moments,** you would find that the journey to understanding becomes a binding glue, and that willingness is what separates the divorcees from long-lasting marriages.

Neisha Guy is from Trinidad and Tobago. Since she can remember, every time someone asked her *What do you want to be when you grow up?* she always responded with *I want to be a Veterinarian.*

She is in love with domesticated animals, but life took her to music and she loves being a singer/songwriter. Her biggest accomplishment publicly is winning *Digicel Rising Stars in 2014*. Her biggest personal achievement is the potential to forgive those who have wronged her repeatedly.

Connect with Neisha Guy:

Facebook1: fb.com/neisha.justis.guy

Facebook2: fb.com/NJustisG

Instagram: instagram.com/neishaguy

Meet the Author

Noreen N. Henry

One of my challenges was emotional eating that progressed into an unhealthy relationship with food. My eating disorder developed as a result of being broken and unhappy. I used food as a numbing device.

I struggled with emotional eating for many years. However, there is always hope, always a solution.

I overcame emotional eating by gaining the right knowledge about it. I read books, completed workbooks, and eventually got coaching. I chose to overcome this dreaded disease.

One of my expectations from a partner is to be highly spiritual. My partner also needs to have a growth mindset. As the Word of God says, two can't walk unless they agree. I'm a life-long learner and will need to have a partner that is on the same page. It doesn't make sense to be with just anyone because if your partner isn't on the same page, there will be major issues from the start.

If someone is struggling with communication, something isn't right to begin with. We make choices due to a lack of knowledge. With that being said, someone struggling with communication in their relationship will need to work on their internal self to overcome that. Start by seeing a coach to get to the root of the struggle and then gain tools to help.

Noreen N. Henry, a Victorious Living Strategist, was born in London, England, and migrated to the U.S. at the tender age of 17. She is passionate about seeing lives transformed from defeat to victory through her *Victorious Living Culture* programs.

As a result of the many trials and tribulations she endured, Noreen learned the tools to be victorious and that she can have joy, peace, and happiness amid chaos while overcoming. She is a multiple #1 international best-seller, coach, speaker, and trainer. Noreen has three children and four grandchildren and resides in New York City, New York, U.S.

Connect with Noreen N. Henry:

Website: NoreenNHenry.com

Instagram: instagram.com/victoriousnoreen

Facebook: fb.com/Noreen.n.henry

Meet the Author

Monica Reed

On the brink of a divorce, I realized that I was the main contributor to my marriage failure. I had carried over childhood experiences and those experiences were showing up in my marriage.

Accepting that I needed healing, I was able to save my marriage. First, I went back to identify who I was. Once I discovered her, I was able to move forward and built the family that I longed for.

One of my expectations of a partner is to be able to embrace all of me: the good, bad, ugly, and loving versions of me. My non-negotiable is someone who lies.

I am in a real open and honest state of life where I have no room for a partner who will not be real and open with me. Thank God he sent me my King when He did.

I would advise those struggling with communication in their relationships that communication is the #1 key in a relationship. Many people believe that if they say less it's best. However, it's when you say more of the right things that you truly build a stronger relationship. Get to a place where you can sit down, effectively communicate, and watch your relationship grow beyond measures. Don't be scared to become vulnerable, just speak.

Monica Reed is a proud mother of four, an award-winning 10x author, transformational speaker, relationship, and business consultant from Ewing, New Jersey, U.S.

Monica started her journey as an entrepreneur by sharing her personal journey with the world. Her story led to reconciliation and healing for many families.

Monica launched her life coaching business and speaking career serving those passionate about sharing their journey. She pledges to spend the rest of her life creating platforms to help entrepreneurs rise, building strong family foundations, and helping more women find their voices, leading them to speak, teach and reach back to pull another woman up.

Connect with Monica Reed:

Website: monicadreed.com

Instagram: instagram.com/monicadreed

Facebook: fb.com/monicareedspeak

Meet the Author

Vernae Taylor

I'm still overcoming one of the greatest tragedies of my life: the loss of my father. I permitted myself to feel every emotion and worked through each stage of grief. I took time to reflect and redefine my identity. While leaning on my faith in God, I documented my progress and began to write the vision for my life, proclaiming that each day that I have breath, his legacy will live on through me.

My most important expectation of a partner is respect! I'm not willing to negotiate my partner not having a personal relationship with God and Jesus Christ.

Also, he has to believe in the institution and covenant of marriage. He has to be able to effectively communicate with me and always have a willingness to try, improve, and learn. He has to be one who can both stimulate my intellect and arouse my humor.

The best advice I would give to a person struggling with communication in his or her relationship is that the greatest key to communication is active listening. Review what your partner is saying versus what you may be hearing and ask yourself if the two align. Another great tool is writing a letter to your partner in difficult scenarios and taking time to unpack it after the exchange. Lastly, praying together and seeking an entity outside of the relationship for guidance, be it a counselor, experienced friend, or a couple is helpful.

Vernae Taylor is the NJ-based Founder/CEO of Triple Threat Vision, LLC, which specializes in mentorship. She is also the Inspirational CEO nominee of *Who's Who of 2020* for the Urban CEO Network and has since adopted the title of *Authorpreneur.*

Vernae has co-authored the following publications:

- The Actor's Side Hustle, Potpourri From the Heart
- Break Through (alongside Les Brown)
- The Evolution Effect
- Our Truth is Not a Lie
- Life of an Entrepreneur 4th Edition

In one of her most meaningful releases, *Letters to my Father - 7 Steps to Healing From the Loss of a Parent*, Vernae empowers people to move from a place of loss or grief, step into their confidence, and dare to live life with purpose. She has appeared in the National Tour of *Almost Heaven: Songs of John Denver*, *Balance of Love* in Atlantic City; the "Tony Award-Winning" musical, *Another Chance*; "Short Film of the Year," *Zahra and the Oil Man;* and was the writer and lead in the award-winning short, *Girl in the Mirror*.

Vernae's recent endeavors include the weekly *Build Your Own Empire* mastermind group on Clubhouse; a collaborative anthology, *Your Voice Matters,* and the development of Breakthrough Network and Life of an Entrepreneur.

Connect with Vernae Taylor:

Website: mylifelivedonpurpose.com

Instagram: instagram.com/vernaetaylor

Facebook: fb.com/vernaeltaylor

www.ingramcontent.com/pod-product-compliance
Lightning Source LLC
Chambersburg PA
CBHW071456070526
44578CB00001B/364